Bowmar/Noble Handwriting F

Reviewers

Sister Andrew Maureen, I. H. M.
Principal
Somerdale, New Jersey

Dr. Fred Chavez
Specialist, Elementary Reading
Los Angeles, California

Beverly Ellis
Elementary Language Arts Supervisor
Springfield, Missouri

Otis H. Lovelace, Jr.
Principal
Charlotte County, Virginia

Dr. Philip Mann
Professor of Psychology
University of Miami, Florida

Dr. Virginia S. Melton
College of Education
Louisiana Tech University, Louisiana

Jeannie Russell
Instructional Specialist
Rosemead, California

Sister Kathleen T. Sullivan
District Superintendent
Staten Island, New York

Mary Janet Taylor
Director of Elementary Instruction
Blytheville, Arkansas

Sister Mary Theiss
Curriculum Coordinator
Milwaukee, Wisconsin

McGraw-Hill School Division

1200 Northwest 63rd Street
Oklahoma City, Oklahoma 73116-5712

Cover Illustration: Mike Wimmer
Illustrations: Clovis Martin

ISBN 0-07-375766-7
ISBN 0-8372-4063-8

40 LKV 25

PRE-TEST

As the sun rises and moves across the United States, people begin to wake up. They get up in Queens, New York, and Roanoke, Virginia, and in East Liverpool and Xenia, Ohio. The sun moves west to Villa Park and Zion, Illinois, and to Great Bend, Kansas. Dawn comes to Dallas, Texas, to Jackson Hole, Wyoming, and Albuquerque, New Mexico. Morning comes to Flagstaff, Arizona, Ventura, California, and Honolulu, Hawaii.

Directions: Copy the paragraph.

CURSIVE ALPHABET

Models of all the cursive letters and numerals are presented on this page.

Aa Bb Cc Dd Ee

Ff Gg Hh Ii Jj

Kk Ll Mm Nn Oo

Pp Qq Rr Ss Tt

Uu Vv Ww Xx Yy Zz

1 2 3 4 5 6 7 8 9 10

Directions: Copy the letters and numerals.

a

SMALL LETTERS

Small **a** is shaped like an oval. It is as tall as the guideline.

a a a aaaaa award

appeal arrange alarm

Always close the oval in small a.

b

Small **b** has a tall upper loop. Small **b** curves up almost to the top line.

b b b bbbbb barbecue

barber bubble blackboard

The lower loop of b curves in slightly.

 DIRECTIONS: Copy the letters, words, and sentences.

c c

Small **c** begins with a short slanted line when it is the first letter in a word.

c c c ccccc choice

commence check connect

Keep small c well rounded.

d

Small **d** is taller than most small letters, but it is not as tall as small **b**.

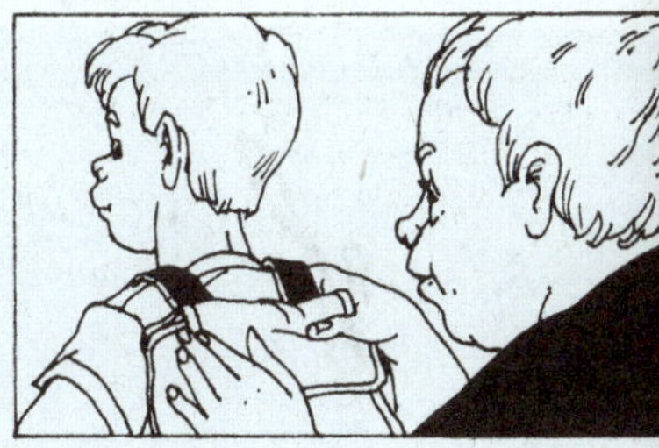

d d d ddddd diamond

deed depend defend

Keep the stem in small d closed.

Directions: Copy the letters, words, and sentences.

e

SMALL LETTERS

Small e curves up from the baseline and around in a loop.

e e eeee every eleven

enemy entirely erase

Always keep the loop in small e open.

f

The lower loop of f reaches almost one-half space below the guideline.

f f f fffff fifteen

off offer officer

Keep the loops of small f open.

 Directions: Copy the letters, words, and sentences.

g

Above the baseline, small **g** is just like small **a**.

g g g ggggg going gang

garage geography geese

Cross the loop of g at the baseline.

h

Small **h** curves up almost to the top line. It has a tall upper loop and a rounded hill.

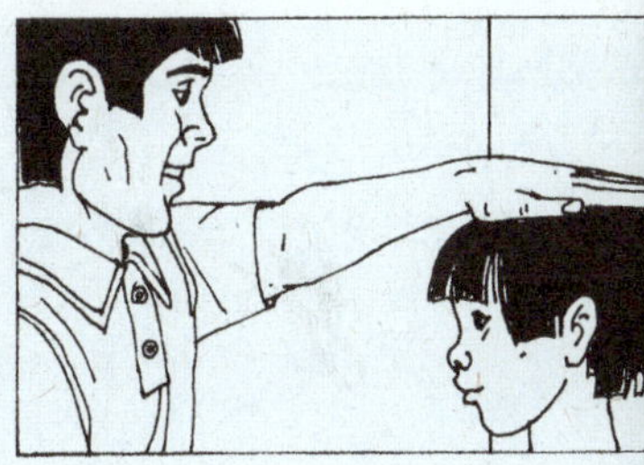

h h h hhhhh height

hatch hitch health

Keep the hill in small h rounded.

Directions: Copy the letters, words, and sentences.

i

SMALL LETTERS

Small **i** is a pointed letter. It is dotted after all the letters in a word are written.

i i dot i iiii insist

invitation inquire information

Keep the stem in small i closed.

j

Small **j** is another pointed letter.

j j dot j jjjj justice

juice junior judge

Always remember to dot small j.

 Directions: Copy the letters, words, and sentences.

k

Small **k** has a tall upper loop. The small loop is written just under the guideline.

k k k k kkkkk kick

knock knuckle knack

Be sure your k's don't look like h's.

l

Small **l** curves up almost to the top line, around in a loop, and down in a slant.

l l lllll lonely little

lullaby lovely ladle

Keep the loop in small l open.

Directions: Copy the letters, words, and sentences.

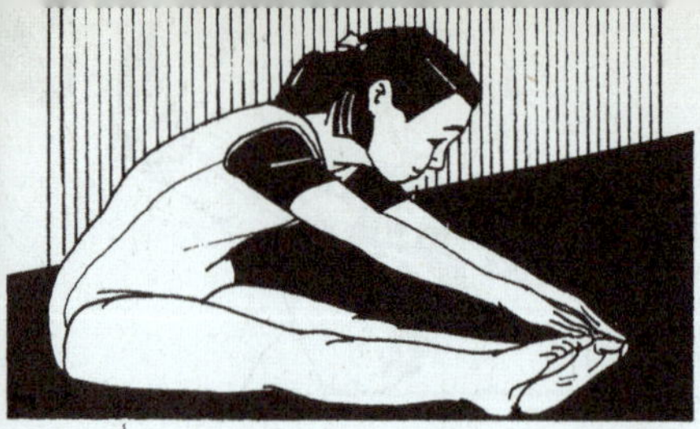

CONNECTIVES

Connectives join letters together to form words. They also set the spacing between the letters in words.

Under-curve connectives

relief luck learn must

niece turn cellar steel

We settled the discussion.

Over-curve connectives

inside danger rang safe

sandy land scene machine

The next exercise is easy.

Directions: Copy the words and sentences.

Long under-curve and long over-curve connectives

jump junior glory zero

jam jar yard gate

My brother is a junior in college.

Connectives from the baseline

first please paid quiz

quantity finish friend

Check your papers carefully.

Directions: Copy the words and sentences.

IMPROVING HANDWRITING: SIZE

Checking your letters for size will help you to improve your handwriting. Straight lines drawn with a ruler should just touch the tops of your letters.

The capital letters are almost a full space high.

Where is the Gulf of Mexico?

The letters **b, f, h, k,** and **l** are as tall as capital letters.

It is better to learn late than never.

The letters **d, p,** and **t** are two-thirds of a space high.

Each student prepared a report.

All the other small letters are one-third of a space high.

The meeting is in the auditorium.

Directions: Copy the sentences. Use a ruler as you check for size.

IMPROVING HANDWRITING: SLANT

Checking your letters for slant will help you to improve your handwriting. Dashed lines drawn through the downstrokes of your letters should be parallel and slanted.

The capital letter downstrokes are slanted and parallel.

Hawaii and Alaska are states.

Part of the small letter downstroke is a straight, slanted line.

Only the ignorant despise education.

The slanted downstrokes should be slanted in the same direction.

America is a land of opportunity.

The Handwriting Guide Sheet can be used to check slant.

Well begun is half done.

Directions: Copy the sentences. Use a ruler as you check for slant.

USING HANDWRITING: PARAGRAPH

The first line of a paragraph is always indented with a space as wide as a capital **O**.

Judo

People of almost any age or size can learn the sport of judo. A judo expert can often win in a contest with a larger and stronger person. Judo was first used by ancient warriors. Later judo was changed so that it was not so rough and dangerous. It became an Olympic sport in 1964.

 Directions: Copy the paragraph.

USING HANDWRITING: POEM

In this poem, each line begins with a capital letter and every other line is indented.

Little Things

Little drops of water,
    Little grains of sand,
Make the mighty ocean
    And the pleasant land.
Thus the little minutes
    Humble though they be,
Make the mighty ages
    Of eternity.
        Ebenezer Cobham Brewer

Directions: Copy the poem.

IMPROVING HANDWRITING: WATCH-OUT LETTERS

When small **a, b, d, e, h,** and **i** are not carefully formed, they may look like other letters.

Keep the oval in small **a** closed at the top.

a a a aaaaa aaaaa aaaaa

Keep the end stroke of small **b** close to the guideline.

b b b bbbbb bbbbb bbbbb

Keep the oval of small **d** closed at the stem.

d d d ddddd ddddd ddddd

regard brand debate

The black dog chased the brown cat.

Directions: Copy the letters, words, and sentence.

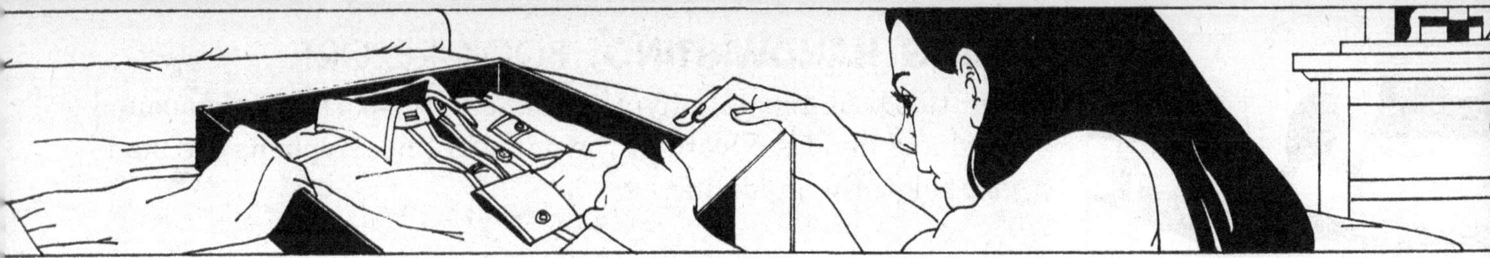

Keep the loop in small **e** open.

e e eeee eeee eeee

Keep the hill in small **h** well rounded.

h h h hhhhh hhhhh hhhhh

Keep the top of small **i** pointed. Remember to dot the letter.

i i i i iiiii iiiii iiiii

chief dishonest children

She has a new linen shirt.

Directions: Copy the letters, words, and sentence.

USING HANDWRITING: BOOK REPORT

In this book report, a hyphen connects the parts of a compound word and divides a word at the end of a line. Hyphens are made just below the guideline.

<u>On the Gold Rush Trail</u>
by Margaret Valentine

When the Grant family sets out
from Iowa in their covered wagon, they
follow the trail of the forty-niners to
California. The two children, Tim and
Betsy, look forward to the trip. They
think the journey will be great fun.
In the spring of 1850, they begin
following the Platte River across
the Great Plains.

The children soon find that the
Gold Rush Trail holds many dangers.
There are roaring rivers, dust storms,
prairie fires, deserts, and mountains.
There are also many wonderful new
things to learn about. They learn
that it's not easy to travel two thou-
sand miles to find a new home. Most
important, they learn that they
are much stronger and smarter than
they realized.

 Directions: Copy the book report.

PROGRESS PAGES

ache aide algae

babble behalf barge

cable called deed

dial eel each

flake flea fled

gill glee glide

Directions: Copy the words.

hall heel high

iced icicle jade

jacks lad leak

life beach click

child birch chalk

bleach faded checked

Directions: Copy the words.

MANUSCRIPT ALPHABET

Manuscript writing is useful in preparing posters, labels, signs, greeting cards, and charts.

Aa Bb Cc Dd Ee Ff

Gg Hh Ii Jj Kk Ll

Mm Nn Oo Pp Qq Rr

Ss Tt Uu Vv Ww Xx

Yy Zz

1 2 3 4 5 6 7 8 9 10

Happy Holidays Happy New Year

Happy Birthday Get Well Soon

Directions: Copy the letters, numerals, and greetings.

USING HANDWRITING: PARAGRAPH

In both manuscript and cursive handwriting, hyphens are made just below the guideline. Quotation marks are written just under the top line.

"Old Faithful"

"Old Faithful" is a geyser in Yellow-
stone National Park. A geyser is a
spring that shoots up hot water with
great force. "Old Faithful" erupts for
about four minutes every sixty-five
minutes. This geyser has earned
its name because it has never
failed to erupt since it was discovered
in 1870.

Directions: Copy the paragraph using manuscript handwriting.

m

SMALL LETTERS

Small **m** has three hills. All the rounded tops are the same height.

m m m m mmmmmm memo

memory museum monument

Keep the hills in small m rounded.

n

Small **n** has two hills. The rounded tops are the same height.

n n n nnnnn none

northern napkin nation

Keep the hills in small n rounded.

Directions: Copy the letters, words, and sentences.

o

The second stroke of small **o** forms a loop at the top of the letter.

o o o ooooo onion

opinion opposite occasion

Keep the end stroke of small o high.

p

The top of small **p** is pointed. The lower loop reaches almost one-half space below the baseline.

p p p p ppppp popular

photograph prompt property

Small p is as tall as small t and d.

Directions: Copy the letters, words, and sentences.

SMALL LETTERS

q

Above the baseline small **q** is shaped like small **a** and **g**.

q q q q qqqqq quick

quiet quotation quotient

The loop of q turns to the right.

r

The second stroke of small **r** slants back down to form a point.

r r r r rrrrr rare

repair radiator require

The point of r goes over the guideline.

 Directions: Copy the letters, words, and sentences.

s

Small **s** has a point just above the guideline.

1 2 3 s sssss suppose

satisfy scissors sense

Keep the top of small s pointed.

t

Small **t** is taller than most small letters. The across stroke is written just above the guideline.

1 2 across t tttt tent

taste tenth thirsty

Keep the stem of small t closed.

Directions: Copy the letters, words, and sentences.

u

SMALL LETTERS

The tops of small **u** are pointed. The bottom of the letter is rounded.

u u u u uuuuuu usual

useful unjust unhurt

Keep the tops of small u pointed.

v

Small **v** begins with a hill. The bottom of the letter is rounded.

v v v vvvv velvet

vacant various voyage

Keep the end stroke of small v high.

Directions: Copy the letters, words, and sentences.

w

Small **w** is pointed at the top. All three points are the same height.

1 2 3 4

w w w w w wwwww window

weather watermelon westward

Keep the tops of small w pointed.

x

Small **x** begins with a hill. The letter is crossed after all the letters in a word are written.

1 slant across

x x x xxxxx fix

excitement expense extra

Always remember to cross your x's.

Directions: Copy the letters, words, and sentences.

y

SMALL LETTERS

Small **y** begins with a hill. The lower loop of small **y** loops up to the left.

y y yyyyy yearly

young yawn yesterday

Complete the lower loop of your y's.

z

Small **z** starts with a hill that ends at the baseline.

z z zzzzz zest

zero zone zipper

Keep the lower loop of z curved.

 Directions: Copy the letters, words, and sentences.

USING HANDWRITING: PARAGRAPH

This paragraph contains all the cursive small letters of the alphabet. The hyphen is made just below the guideline.

Animal Quiz

During our visit to the zoo, we enjoyed watching some unusual birds that looked like roly-poly little men in dress suits. These birds had short, flipper-like wings, but they couldn't fly. They were excellent swimmers, but waddled around quite comically when they tried to walk. Can you name them?

Directions: Copy the paragraph.

BRIDGE CONNECTIVES

Bridge connectives join small **b, o, v,** and **w** with letters that begin at the guideline.

oar occupy row warm

room vanity wonder vacuum

The rocket zoomed across the sky.

walrus vocal bark oasis

valley boast won oatmeal

I watched them paint the van.

 Directions: Copy the words and sentences.

HORIZONTAL CONNECTIVES

Horizontal connectives join small **b, o, v,** and **w** with letters that begin at the baseline.

wear every bench oval

shoe best weekly average

We've been reading poetry in class.

brittle comb broken order

oval bread omit brow

That brush has sharp bristles.

Directions: Copy the words and sentences.

USING HANDWRITING: COMPOSITION

In a composition, the first line of each paragraph is indented. In this composition, the title is centered on the line with a blank line following.

Mary Cassatt

Mary Cassatt was a famous American artist, but she spent most of her life in France. She was born in 1845 in Pittsburgh and studied art in America. In 1868, she went to live in Paris. She got many new ideas about art from the French artists.

Mary is best known for her paintings of mothers and children doing everyday things together. Like many artists of her time, she admired the soft, clear colors and delicate lines of Oriental paintings. When you find a Mary Cassatt painting in a gallery, you'll see mothers and children painted in beautiful colors.

Directions: Copy the composition.

IMPROVING HANDWRITING: SHAPE

Checking your letters for shape by comparing them to correctly formed models will help you to improve your handwriting.

The ovals in **a, d, g, q,** and **o** should be closed at the top.

My dog learned the trick quickly.

The tops of **i, j, u, w, t, p, r, d,** and **s** should be pointed.

The audience watched with interest.

The loops of **b, e, f, h, k,** and **l** should be open.

Birds of a feather flock together.

The hills and valleys of **m, n, v, y,** and **x** should be well rounded.

I expect to hear from you soon.

Directions: Copy the sentences and check your handwriting for shape.

IMPROVING HANDWRITING: SPACING WORDS

Checking the spacing between words will help you to improve your handwriting. The space between words should be as wide as a small **o.**

My compass belongs inside that case.

Mrs. Lopez planted peas and beans.

John has a government job now.

She will bring your book tomorrow.

Indra is taking flute lessons.

Jim is studying the flight of eagles.

Directions: Copy the sentences. Use a ruler as you check for spacing.

USING HANDWRITING: DIARY ENTRY

In this diary, the date of the entry is written in the upper right corner. A blank line follows the date. Quotation marks are placed around the exact words of a speaker.

July 18, 1987

We got up early and went to the airport. At first only a few of us were standing along the fence. Then more and more people came. We stood packed together, looking up into the clear morning sky.

Then someone shouted, "Look! It's Air Force One!" We saw a huge silver plane dropping slowly from the air and touching down on the runway.

There was a great roar as it rolled up in front of us. It stopped. People pushed a stairway up to the door. I held my breath. The big silver door slowly opened. Then out stepped the President of the United States. He raised his hand and waved to all the people. Was I mistaken, or did the President look right at me and smile?

Directions: Copy the diary entry.

IMPROVING HANDWRITING: WATCH-OUT LETTERS

When small **m, n, o, r,** and **t** are not carefully formed, they may look like other letters.

Keep the three hills in small **m** well rounded.

m m mmmmm mmmmm

Keep the two hills in small **n** well rounded.

n n nnnnn nnnnn nnnnn

Keep the end stroke of small **o** close to the guideline.

o o o ooooo ooooo ooooo

enjoyment forgiven lemon

Don is a newcomer to our town.

Directions: Copy the letters, words, and sentence.

Keep the top of small **r** pointed.

r r r r rrrrr rrrrr rrrrr

Keep the stem in small **t** closed. Remember to cross the letter.

t t t t ttttt ttttt ttttt

toward pretzel heart

I'll eat the pear later.

This sentence contains all the watch-out letters.

The brave man stopped the thief.

Directions: Copy the letters, words, and sentences.

USING HANDWRITING: PARAGRAPH

This paragraph contains the eleven watch-out letters you have been practicing.

What Is an Echo?

When a noise is made, sound waves travel through the air in all directions. We first hear the sound when these waves reach our ears. If the sound waves also hit some large object such as the side of a building, they bounce back and may reach our ears a second time. This second sound is called an echo.

 Directions: Copy the paragraph.

USING HANDWRITING: TALL TALE

The first line of a paragraph is always indented with a space as wide as a capital **O.**

Marta was the strongest, fastest girl I ever met. She could balance 5000 pounds, and was faster than the wind. When Marta was thirsty, she emptied a lake and ate the fish as a snack.

Marta was also very brave. One day, Marta saw a fallen bridge. A bus was hanging over the edge of the bridge. Marta

Directions: Copy the beginning of this tall tale. Write your own ending.

PROGRESS PAGES

most now ours

pours quote row

stopper trust utter

vow woven anxious

youth zoom stove

moon post morn

 Directions: Copy the words.

not toys upper

outer voter woolly

purrs excuse yours

quiz size topaz

roost stow zone

snooze move acquaint

Directions: Copy the words.

USING HANDWRITING: POSTER

Proper names and important words in titles are always capitalized. The first word of a sentence is also capitalized.

Independence Day

The Declaration of Independence was adopted on July 4, 1776. Our first Independence Day was celebrated in Philadelphia on July 8, 1776. The Declaration was read to the people and the Liberty Bell was rung. Since then, we have observed this holiday every year on July 4.

Directions: Copy the poster.

A O D C

CAPITAL LETTERS

Capital **A, O, D,** and **C** curve around to the left.

A A A Akemi August

O O O Oregon Oliver

D D D D Denver Dutch

C C C Carmen Canada

Columbus reached America in 1492.

Did you study about the Orient?

Directions: Copy the letters, words, and sentences.

E P R B

Capital **E** begins with a loop and curves around to the left. Capital **P, R,** and **B** begin with a slanted stroke.

E Europe Ellis

P Patrick Philip

R R Roberto Ravi

B B B Boston Blanca

Polo is a popular sport in England.

Both Rosa and Pam like the game.

Directions: Copy the letters, words, and sentences.

F T S G

CAPITAL LETTERS

Capital **F** and **T** begin with a reverse curve. Capital **S** and **G** begin with a curve up from the baseline.

1 2 3 4 5 F Finland Florida

1 2 3 4 T Teresa Turkey

1 2 3 S Sweden Sumi

1 2 3 4 G Geneva Greece

San Francisco is in California.

Ted and Gerry are going there soon.

Directions: Copy the letters, words, and sentences.

I J L Q

Capital **I** begins at the baseline. Capital **J** begins just under the baseline. Capital **L** and **Q** have strokes that curve below the baseline.

I I I I Iowa Ireland

J J J Janet Juan

L L L L London Lan

Q Q Q Q Quebec Quica

Laura will visit Japan in July.

Queen Isabella sponsored Columbus.

Directions: Copy the letters, words, and sentences.

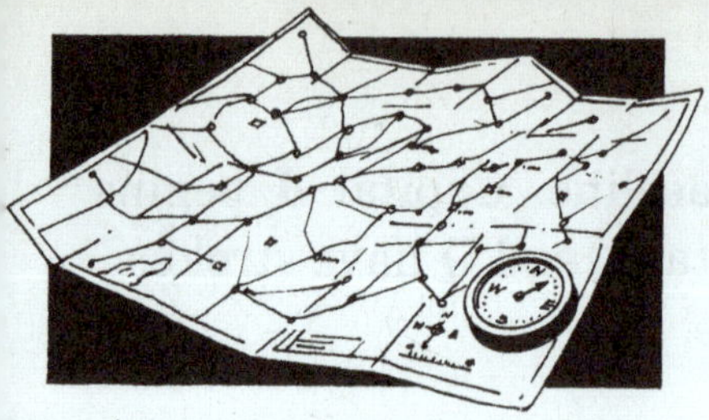

USING HANDWRITING: MATH PROBLEMS

In math problems, the numerals are often lined up in columns and rows.

$$\begin{array}{r} 682 \\ +9143 \\ \hline 9825 \end{array} \qquad \begin{array}{r} 168 \\ +79 \\ \hline 247 \end{array} \qquad \begin{array}{r} 4629 \\ +215 \\ \hline \end{array}$$

$$\begin{array}{r} 2345 \\ +9876 \\ \hline 12,221 \end{array} \qquad \begin{array}{r} \$87.96 \\ -62.54 \\ \hline \end{array} \qquad \begin{array}{r} 3476 \\ \times 8 \\ \hline \end{array}$$

$25 + 75 = 100$ $\qquad 88 - 34 =$

$69 \times 10 = 690$ $\qquad 639 \div 3 =$

Directions: Copy and solve the problems.

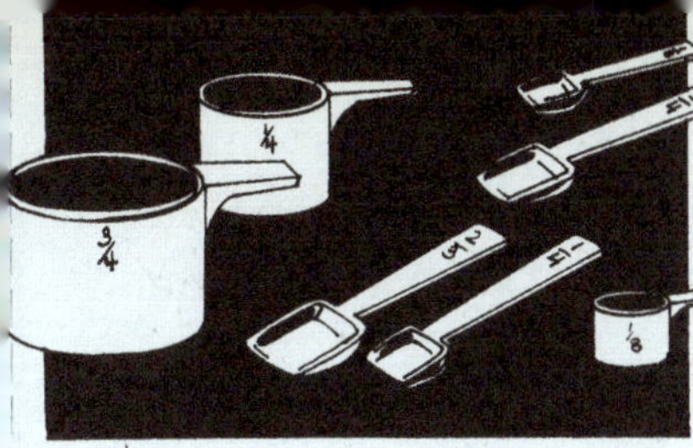

USING HANDWRITING: MATH PROBLEMS

Fractions show numbers less than **1.** The numerals in fractions are a little less than one-third of a space high.

$$\begin{array}{r} \frac{3}{5} \\ -\frac{1}{5} \\ \hline \frac{4}{5} \end{array} \qquad \begin{array}{r} \frac{4}{16} \\ -\frac{7}{16} \\ \hline \end{array} \qquad \begin{array}{r} 1\frac{2}{9} \\ +2\frac{6}{9} \\ \hline \end{array}$$

$$\begin{array}{r} \frac{4}{10} \\ -\frac{3}{10} \\ \hline \frac{1}{10} \end{array} \qquad \begin{array}{r} \frac{7}{15} \\ -\frac{5}{15} \\ \hline \end{array} \qquad \begin{array}{r} 6\frac{13}{24} \\ -4\frac{6}{24} \\ \hline \end{array}$$

$\frac{2}{2} = 1$ $\qquad \frac{4}{4} = 1$ $\qquad \frac{16}{16} =$ $\qquad \frac{5}{5} =$

$\frac{2}{4} = \frac{1}{2}$ $\qquad \frac{12}{16} = \frac{3}{4}$ $\qquad \frac{6}{8} =$ $\qquad \frac{4}{16} =$

Directions: Copy and solve the problems.

IMPROVING HANDWRITING: ALIGNMENT

Checking the alignment of your letters will help you to improve your handwriting. Aligned letters should sit on a straight line drawn through the bases of your letters.

Time and tide wait for no one.

Jerry has a jumping frog.

Honesty is the best policy.

Larry is reading about Don Quixote.

We saw the lions at the zoo.

Rosa ate lunch with her friend.

Directions: Copy the sentences. Use a ruler as you check for alignment.

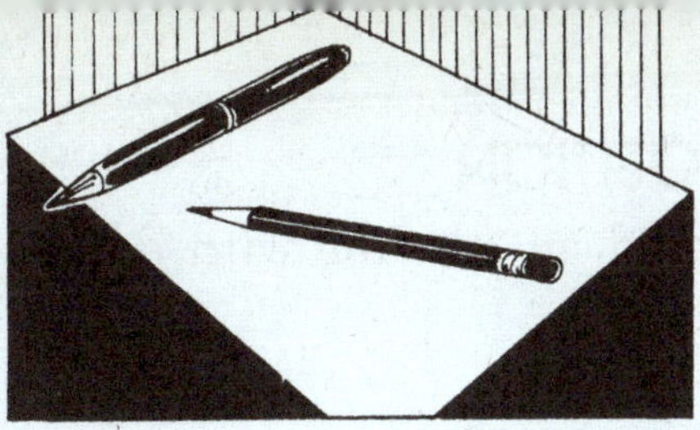

IMPROVING HANDWRITING: OVERALL APPEARANCE

Checking the overall appearance of your written work will help you to improve your handwriting. A paper should have even margins and neat handwriting.

(Use Your Name) (Use Today's Date)

Skip a line

(Title of the Paragraph)

Skip a line

In 1620, the Pilgrims came to America. During their first winter in Massachusetts, many died from the cold and lack of food. When spring arrived, they planted crops which would supply them with food for the coming winter.

Directions: Copy the paragraph. Check the overall appearance of your paper.

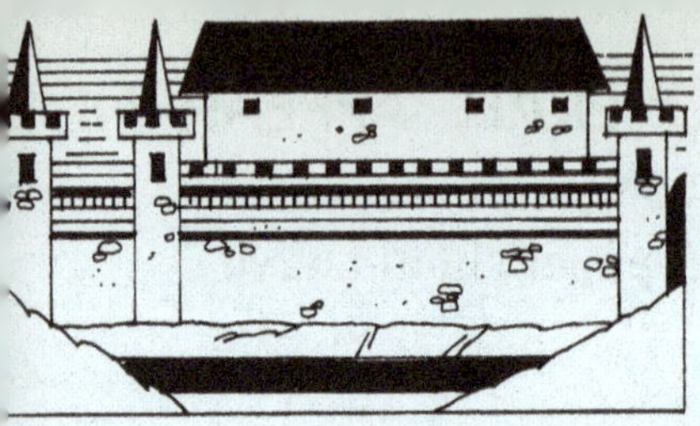

USING HANDWRITING: COMPOSITION

The title of this composition is centered on the line with a blank line below.

Tapestries

Would you like to have lived in the Middle Ages? Would you like to have called an old castle your home? You might have found living in a castle quite uncomfortable! The castles were often cold, dark, and damp. To help keep the heat inside, large cloths were sometimes hung on castle walls. Some of these cloths, called tapestries, had colored pictures stitched on them.

Because colors look different in sunlight and moonlight, the colors of the threads in the tapestries sometimes appeared to change in a strange way. On a moonlit night, animals or persons stitched into the tapestry might seem to disappear into the shadows. In the brightness of the morning sunlight, however, they would reappear again, as if by magic!

Directions: Copy the composition.

IMPROVING HANDWRITING: WATCH-OUT NUMERALS

Be careful: **5's** can look like **3's**
6's can look like **0's**
7's can look like **1's**

Start the last stroke of **5** where you began the numeral.

5 5 5 55555 55555 55555

Keep the loop in **6** between the guideline and the baseline.

6 6 66666 66666 66666

Keep the downstroke of **7** straight and slanted to the left.

7 7 7 77777 77777 77777

I live at 657 Summit Avenue.

Mrs. Chin collected 567 buttons.

Directions: Copy the numerals and sentences.

USING HANDWRITING: TABLE

In this table, the words in the left column are lined up on the left. The numerals in the right column are lined up on the right.

Calorie Table

1 apple	117
1 banana	176
1 slice of bread	63
1 carrot	42
1 serving of peas	56
1 tablespoon of butter	100
1 glass of milk	166
1 orange	68
1 hamburger	350
1 T-bone steak	235

Directions: Copy the table.

USING HANDWRITING: TABLE

In this table, the title is centered. The equal signs in the table are also centered and lined up in a column.

Measurements of Length

12 inches	=	1 foot
3 feet	=	1 yard
5280 feet	=	1 mile
1760 yards	=	1 mile
3 miles	=	1 league
10 millimeters	=	1 centimeter
100 centimeters	=	1 meter
1000 meters	=	1 kilometer
100 meters	=	1 hectometer

Directions: Copy the table.

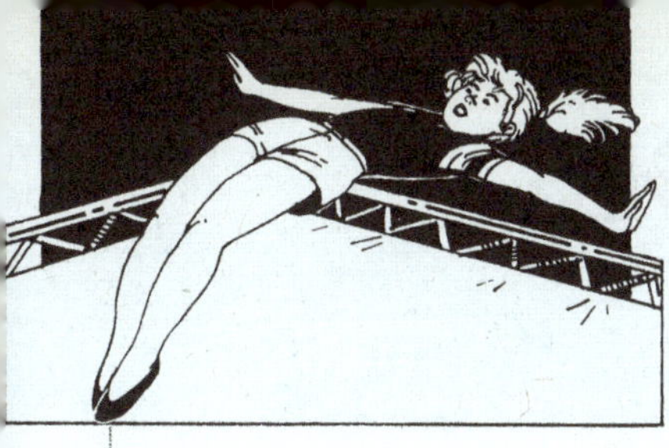

USING HANDWRITING: PARAGRAPH

In this paragraph, the title is centered on the line with a blank line below.

Trampoline Records

Trampolines were first used by entertainers in 1910. A sport trampoline was invented in 1936. World Championships were first held in 1964. In 1974, a team of 6 jumped on a trampoline for 1248 hours (52 days). A solo record was set in 1980 by a girl who kept bouncing for 240 hours!

Directions: Copy the paragraph using cursive handwriting.

PROGRESS PAGES

Inventor Robert Fulton was born in 1765 and died in 1815.

Elisha G. Otis invented the first safe elevator in 1852.

Quite a few years later, the genius Charles P. Steinmetz was born.

Alexander Graham Bell's voice was first heard on the telephone in 1875.

Directions: Copy the sentences.

Thomas Alva Edison perfected the electric light bulb in 1879.

Charles F. Jenkins invented the first film projector in 1894.

Alexander De Seversky developed fighter plane designs in the 1930's.

The self-developing camera was invented by Edwin H. Land.

Directions: Copy the sentences.

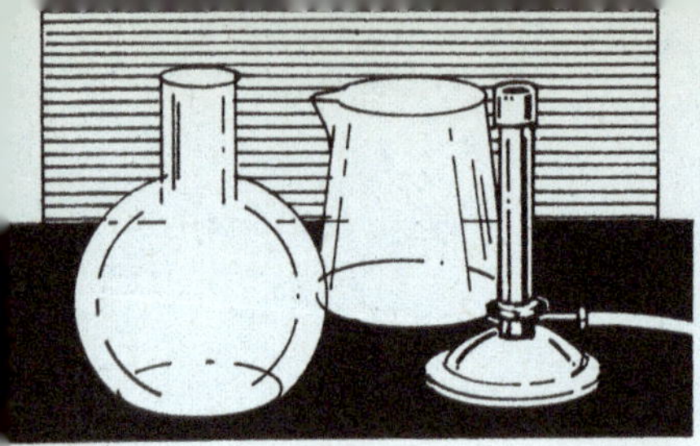

USING HANDWRITING: NUMBERED LIST

The items in this list are numbered. The numerals are lined up on the left, one under the other.

Preparing a Science Exhibit.

1. Get suggestions.
2. Choose an idea.
3. Do background reading.
4. Take notes.
5. Build the equipment.
6. Label the equipment.
7. Plan the demonstration.
8. Make charts and diagrams.
9. Set up an exhibit.

 Directions: Copy the list.

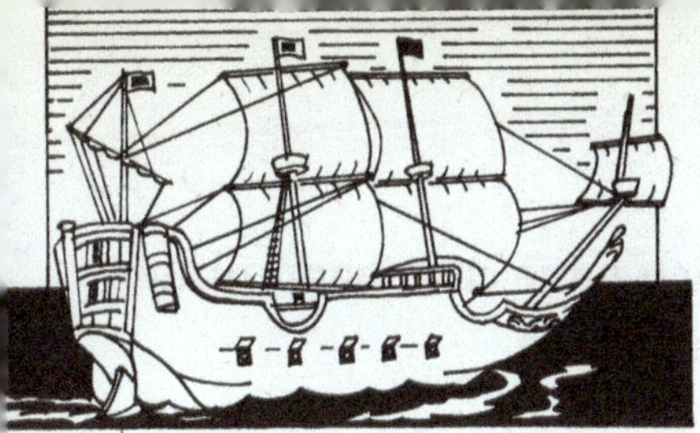

USING HANDWRITING: TABLE

In this table, the information is shown in two columns. The title is centered and the words in each column are lined up on the left.

Famous Explorers

Alexander the Great	Macedonian
Eric the Red	Norwegian
Marco Polo	Italian
Christopher Columbus	Italian
Amerigo Vespucci	Italian
Hernando Cortes	Spanish
Juan Ponce de Leon	Spanish
Sir Francis Drake	English
Ferdinand Magellan	Portuguese

Directions: Copy the table.

H K M N

CAPITAL LETTERS

Capitals **H, K, M,** and **N** each have cane beginnings. Each letter begins with a small loop.

H Holland Henry

K Kathy Kansas

M Michigan March

N Nevada Nancy

The Hudson River is in New York.

Kansas City is in Missouri.

Directions: Copy the letters, words, and sentences.

U V Y

Capitals **U, V,** and **Y** each have cane beginnings. The second stroke for each letter curves around and down in a slant.

1 2 3 U Utah Una Ursula

1 2 V Verrazano Vidya

1 2 3 Y Yellowstone York

Utah is named after the Ute Indians.

Venice has many canals.

The Yukon has a cold climate.

Directions: Copy the letters, words, and sentences.

W X Z

CAPITAL LETTERS

Capital **W, X,** and **Z** begin with a small loop.

W W W W W W Wednesday

X X X X X Xavier Xingu

Z Z Z Z Zurich Zelda

The White House is in Washington, D.C.

X rays were an important discovery.

New Zealand is near Australia.

Directions: Copy the letters, words, and sentences.

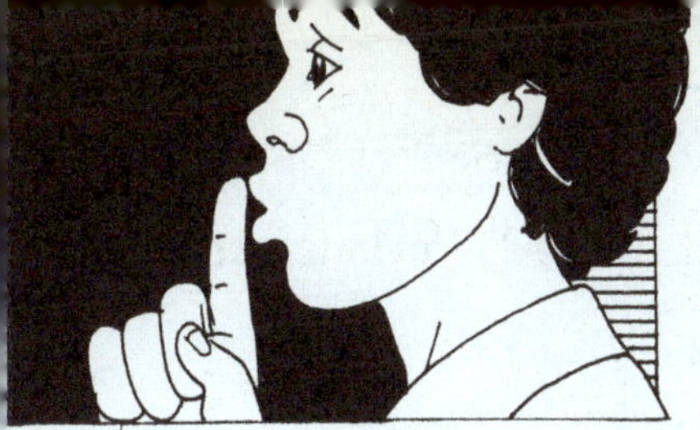

USING HANDWRITING: POEM

In this poem, each line begins with a capital letter and every other line is indented.

Silent Messages

A finger on my lips says "Hush,"
  A wave can say "Hello,"
I clap to say "Hooray for you!"
  I shake my head for "No."

And if I want to tell you "Yes,"
  My head will also nod.
All this I say without a sound.
  I think that's very odd!

Directions: Copy the poem.

ABBREVIATIONS

An abbreviation is a shortened form of a word. Periods are usually placed after abbreviations.

Monday	Mon.
Tuesday	Tues.
Wednesday	Wed.
Thursday	Thurs.
Friday	Fri.
Saturday	Sat.
Sunday	Sun.
dozen	doz.
teaspoon	tsp.
tablespoon	tbsp.
August	Aug.
September	Sept.
October	Oct.
November	Nov.
December	Dec.
January	Jan.
February	Feb.
Boulevard	Blvd.
Avenue	Ave.
Street	St.
Circle	Cir.
Drive	Dr.

Directions: Copy the words and their abbreviations.

USING HANDWRITNG: LIST

In this list, abbreviations are used to save space and the writer's time.

The visiting nurse used abbreviations when she made a list of her calls:

Aug. 28. 10 A.M. 126 N. Main St.
Aug. 28. 2 P.M. 333 E. Balboa Dr.
Aug. 29. 11 A.M. 270 W. Ellis Ln.
Aug. 29. 3 P.M. 109 N. Center St.
Aug. 30. 1 P.M. 20 E. Jefferson Ave
Aug. 31. 10 A.M. 542 S. Clark Dr.
Sept. 1. 2 P.M. 116 W. Linder Ct.
Sept. 2. 11 A.M. 88 N. Maple Rd.

Directions: Copy the list.

USING HANDWRITING: FRIENDLY LETTER

The heading, closing, and signature of this friendly letter all begin in the middle of the line. The greeting begins at the left margin.

Heading { 6721 Lake Drive
Portland, Oregon 97208
March 6, 19__

Dear Helen, } Greeting

I'm sorry to hear that you're sick. I was hoping that we could go to the movies on Saturday. Let me know if you're feeling better.

Closing { Your friend,
Signature { Anthony Peck

Directions: Copy the letter. Use today's date in the heading.

USING HANDWRITING: ADDRESSING AN ENVELOPE

On this envelope, the address of the person sending the letter is in the upper left corner of the envelope. The name and address of the person receiving the letter is in the center.

Anthony Peck
6721 Lake Drive
Portland, Oregon 97208

Miss Helen Marsh
543 Garden Street
Portland, Oregon 97208

Directions: Copy the addresses.

PROGRESS PAGES

When the United States was young, people sang "Yankee Doodle." During the Civil War, people played "Dixie" and "Home Sweet Home" on the pianos in their parlors. Our cowboys sang to their cattle on the prairies. Later, Americans learned songs from the Ziegfield Follies. They listened to Woody Guthrie on the radio.

Directions: Copy the paragraph.

My friends and I have decided to form a reading club. Hilda, Nick, Kent, and Vera are planning to join. We have asked Yetta and Upton to choose some books for us. Xavier will be our secretary and Zelda will be the treasurer. We'll meet once a month at members' homes. Would you like to join us?

Directions: Copy the paragraph.

USING HANDWRITING: COMPOSITION

Developing a smooth rhythm while you write a composition will help you to increase the speed of your handwriting.

Studying the Ocean

Marine biologists are learning
a lot about human beings
from studying animals in the
ocean. Experiments with sea
urchins, horseshoe crabs, and
other creatures have taught
biologists how human bodies work.
It begins when scientists
lower their nets and cameras
into mysterious, deep waters. Far
below the surface are animals
that always live in darkness.
For these animals, there is no
difference between night and day.
Their world has no change
of season or temperature.
Marine biologists need to learn
how these strange animals
find food in the cold, dark
water.

Directions: Copy the composition.

FINAL TEST

The ancient Greeks dreamed of flying. So did Leonardo da Vinci. In 1903 the Wright Brothers of Dayton, OH flew just 120 feet. Quickly and quietly they flew at Kitty Hawk, NC. Up rose their plane, opening the age of flight to valiant pioneers like Chuck Yeager, who broke the sound barrier in the amazing X-1. From there, humans exited Earth. Zooming into space went the proud rockets and spacecraft: Apollo, Jupiter, Redstone, Pioneer, and Mariner.

Directions: Copy the paragraph.

HANDWRITING GUIDE SHEET

The Handwriting Guide Sheet is placed under your writing paper. It is used to check letters for correct slant and to check for uniform spacing between words.